When Someone You Love Is Polyamorous

Also by Elisabeth Sheff

Stories From the Polycule: Real Life in Polyamorous Families
        Thorntree Press, 2015
The Polyamorists Next Door: Inside Multiple-Partner
        Relationships and Families
        Rowman & Littlefield, 2013

When Someone You Love Is Polyamorous

Understanding Poly People and Relationships

Dr. Elisabeth Sheff

Thorntree  Press

Thorntree Press, LLC
P.O. BOX 301231
Portland, OR 97294
press@thorntreepress.com

Cover photo/illustration © vilaxIt/Depositphotos.com
Cover and interior design by Jeff Werner
Substantive editing by Roma Ilnyckyj
Copy-editing by Eve Rickert
Proofreading by Roma Ilnyckyj

Library of Congress Cataloging-in-Publication Data
Names: Sheff, Elisabeth, 1969- author.
Title: When someone you love is polyamorous : a guide to under-
        standing poly people and relationships / Dr. Elisabeth Sheff.
Description: Portland, OR : Thorntree Press, [2016]
Identifiers: LCCN 2016011559 (print) | LCCN 2016015650 (ebook)
        | ISBN 9780996460187 (pbk.) | ISBN 9780996460194 (Epub)
        | ISBN 9781944934101 (Kindle)
Subjects: LCSH: Non-monogamous relationships. | Open marriage.
        | Sexual ethics.
Classification: LCC HQ980 .S533 2016 (print) | LCC HQ980 (ebook)
        | DDC 306.84/23--dc23
LC record available at https://lccn.loc.gov/2016011559

10 9 8 7 6 5 4 3 2

Printed in the United States of America on paper that is certified by the Forest Stewardship Council®and the Rainforest Alliance.

Introduction

Hello, I'm Dr. Elisabeth Sheff, a sociologist and expert on non-traditional relationships. I'll be your guide to learning about polyamory.

I've spent many years studying and presenting on polyamory, and people at my lectures tend to have the same questions: How does polyamory work? What does it mean for women? How will this affect my loved ones? What about kids? My research has provided some of the answers to these questions. In addition, a growing number of books on polyamorous relationships offer insights, and a great deal of information is available online. At the end of the pamphlet, I've listed some resources that can help you find out more.

The information in this pamphlet comes from my study of polyamorous families with children. I interviewed 133 people (including 22 children between ages 5 and 17) over the course of 15 years, from 1996 to 2012. The people in my study were the ones who continued to think of themselves as polyamorous and choose polyamorous relationships, so my data reflect the more optimistic side of polyamory, because it comes from people in (mostly) happy poly families, rather than those who may have tried polyamory and found it didn't work for them. Even so, my findings paint a fairly accurate picture of the ups and downs of daily life in these functional poly families.

I myself am monogamous. When I first learned of the idea of polyamory, I was initially quite bewildered. But over the years, I have come to see it as a legitimate choice that can work very well for people who are honest and communicate with their families' best interests at heart. It doesn't work for me, and it may not work for you. But I have seen it in action and believe that it can create a tremendously loving and happy family life for those who choose it. I hope the information in this pamphlet will be useful as you begin a conversation about polyamory with your loved one.

What is polyamory?

Polyamory is one form of *consensual non-monogamy*. Consensual non-monogamy is an umbrella term for any relationship type in which people are not monogamous. Polyamory emphasizes emotional connection between or among more than two romantic partners who know about (and might even like) each other.

You can see the glossary for a list of polyamory-related terms, but here are a few important words to get us started:

- *polyamorist*: a person who has polyamorous relationships
- *poly*:
  - a short form of the word "polyamorist"
  - an adjective to describe something that has polyamorous qualities (a "poly person" or a "poly relationship")
  - an umbrella term for several different types of non-monogamous relationships

To better understand polyamory, it's helpful to take a look at what it is not. Polyamory is not...

For everyone. Polyamory can be a complex and intense relationship style that takes time and devotion to maintain. Many people prefer the simplicity, security, and exclusivity of monogamy.

Cheating. In polyamorous relationships, everyone is (ideally) aware of the other partners. Relationships have been negotiated with agreements to handle issues like scheduling and safer sex.

Swinging. Swinging tends to focus on sexual variety and puts less emphasis on emotional intimacy with people outside a core couple. Some swingers forbid emotional connection, or even repeated interaction with the same "outside" lover.

Polygamy. In polygamy, people are married to more than one person. Polyamorists are not always married. Even more importantly, polygamy is almost always practiced as *polygyny*, or one man married to multiple women. Usually in those relationships, the women are not allowed to have other male partners, or to have sex with each other. Most polyamorous relationships, in contrast, allow people of all genders to have multiple partners.

Sex addiction. Poly people spend a lot more time communicating about their feelings than they do having sex. For someone whose primary motivation is sex, there are far easier ways to get it than becoming polyamorous.

Group sex. Most often, poly people interact sexually only in pairs.

Do people choose to be poly?

For some people, polyamory is a sexual orientation. For others, it is a lifestyle.

People who experience polyamory as a sexual orientation describe themselves as being "wired" that way. These people say that they have always been oriented toward multiple people in many ways:

- They often did not have a single best friend when they were growing up, but tended to socialize in groups.
- They find it hard to stay in monogamous relationships.
- They felt trapped in monogamous relationships, or they cheated until they stopped making agreements to be monogamous.
- They literally cannot imagine being comfortable in a monogamous relationship.

Folks who are poly by orientation will most likely be in some form of open relationship for the rest of their lives. When people with a poly orientation talk about how they feel in a monogamous relationship, they compare it to wearing shoes that are three sizes too small, or a lesbian trying to be happy in a romantic relationship with a man. They might be able to force themselves into that situation for a while, but it is not sustainable for them without a lot of pain and eventual damage.

For people who experience polyamory as a choice, there is much more flexibility for them to find fulfillment in a range of relationship styles. Some poly-as-lifestyle folks choose to be polyamorous for a portion of their lives: while they are young and do not have children; after a divorce, when they want to play the field in an open and honest way; or after their kids have moved out and they feel more freedom to experiment with their sexuality. Some people who see poly-amory as a lifestyle option choose it for personal and political reasons as a permanent lifestyle, and others go in and out of it depending on what else is happening in their lives.

Traits of polyamorous people

Most people who identify as poly live in Australia, Canada, the United States, and Western Europe. Some live together, usually in groups of two to five, and others live alone, or with roommates. Many poly folks have children, some of them from previous monogamous relationships, and others born into poly households. Women in poly communities tend to be either bisexual or heterosexual, and most men are heterosexual, with a few bisexual people. Poly people tend to be politically liberal.

It is hard to tell how many people are having polyamorous relationships in the United States. First, because of the wide variety of non-monogamous styles, it's difficult to decide whom to count. Also, poly people can be hard to find, because they are often closeted, and there is no mechanism to count them (yet).

Still, a number of estimates exist. The most well-researched one comes from Kelly Cookson, an independent academic. Unfortunately, this estimate only deals with the total number of people who participate in some form of consensual non-monogamy, and there's no way to estimate how many of those identify as polyamorous. In an email to me, Cookson summarized his results:

    ❧   There are millions of sexually non-monogamous couples in the United States.

- Estimates of people who have actually tried sexual non-monogamy (rather than simply being open to it as an idea) are around 1.2 to 2.4 million.
- An estimated 9.8 million people have some kind of agreement with their partner that they can have other lovers. This does not necessarily mean that they have intimate relationships with these other lovers.
- These millions include polyamorists, swingers, and other sexually non-monogamous people.

Monogamy is far more popular in the United States today than is any form of openly conducted non-monogamy. Even among non-monogamies, swinging is far better known and appears to be much more common than polyamory. Clearly, polyamory appeals to a minority of people.

Some personality types are more suited to polyamory. Polyamory can be a good choice for people who relish social interaction, want to examine their feelings and discuss them in detail with others, like trying new things, enjoy sharing, find themselves falling in love with more than one person at a time, have a high sex drive or want sexual variety, are willing to use safer-sex techniques, and are open to the idea of honest non-monogamy.

Other common characteristics that appear to be linked to an interest in polyamory are things like being at least a little geeky, enjoying science fiction, having an interest in kink, working with technology, being economically self-sufficient (or having enough education that you could get a job if you needed to), and thinking of yourself as open-minded.

Why are people polyamorous?

People report a range of reasons they want to be polyamorous.

More love. Pretty much everyone who wants to have a polyamorous relationship is interested in love. Some other forms of consensual non-monogamy, such as swinging, allow people to have sexual variety with little to no emotional involvement, and might require a little less maintenance than the emotional complexity than can come with polyamory. In order to choose the more complex and emotionally intimate style of polyamory, most people find they have to emphasize love over sex.

More needs met. One of the most important things poly people like about their relationships is that they get more—and different—needs met in different relationships. Having multiple partners allows people to go see a play with the partner who loves the arts and go camping with the other partner who is an outdoor enthusiast. That way, the person gets to see plays and go camping, and gets to do it with people who are having fun too, instead of someone who would rather not be there.

Sexual variety. Many people in poly relationships report that they enjoy the sexual variety of being able to have sex with more than one person, without having to give up the relationships they are already enjoying. Being in a loving, stable relationship and still having sex with new people is a big draw for some people interested in polyamory, but not everyone.

Expanded family. Adults and children both experience additional support and connection through polyamorous families. Adults not only have additional partners, but often form connections with their partner's partners, who are called *metamours* in poly lingo. Metamours generally do not have sex with each other, but may develop emotionally intimate relationships that bond them in to an expanded family.

Freedom. Being free from the restrictions of monogamy means not only freedom to experiment with multiple partners, but also freedom to question other norms in our society. This form of critical thinking is not just about questioning monogamy, but also about questioning other things that are often taken for granted, such as what makes a relationship "successful," or whether all relationships need to follow the same, socially prescribed template.

Types of polyamorous relationships

Poly people share a common focus on honesty, emotional intimacy, gender equality, and openness to multiple partners. But the ways in which people actually practice polyamory vary dramatically.

- *Polyfidelity* is a subset of polyamorous relationships in which people expect sexual fidelity among a designated group that is closed unless otherwise explicitly negotiated.
- *Polyaffective* relationships are non-sexual, emotionally intimate relationships between metamours who share a polyamorous partner but are not lovers themselves.
- *Solo polys* or *free agents* have emotionally intimate and lasting relationships, but don't organize their lives around romantic relationships and usually don't identify as part of a couple.
- Some poly people are coupled with or legally married to a *primary partner,* with whom they share a home, finances, and children. These people also date, and often love, people other than their primary partner. These other partners are called *secondary partners*.
- Some poly people reject the implied hierarchy of the primary/secondary model. They emphasize *nesting* (living together) versus *non-nesting* (living separately) relationships.
- Group relationships like *triads* (three-person relationships) or *quads* (four partners) connect multiple adults who may or may not have children or live together.
- *Moresomes* are group relationships with five or more people. Moresomes can merge into *intimate networks* that connect groups of people who share common lovers, exes, and friends.

Most poly people have identified an "emotional band-width," the amount of emotional intimacy, relating, and effort for which they have room in their lives. For some, this translates into a set number of relationships they can handle at any one time: three is a common number. Others seem to have an infinite capacity to form new relationships with other people, and boundless enthusiasm for maintaining them.

Emotional intimacy with multiple partners

For people in monogamous relationships, it can be hard to imagine how polyamorists can nurture emotional connections with multiple partners at the same time. In our society, "settling down" in a monogamous relationship is a sign of maturity. Non-monogamy, in contrast, can appear immature, insincere, and insecure. In reality, some polyamorists say that having relationships outside the norm actually requires a lot communication, honesty, and self-growth.

Communication. Communication is one of the most important features of polyamorous relationships. Poly people rely on good communication to discuss relationship boundaries and safer-sex agreements, express their feelings, and get to know each other. Communication is the main way that poly people build emotional intimacy. Poly folks often enjoy sex, and sexual intimacy can certainly contribute to emotional intimacy, but very few polyamorous (or monogamous) relationships can thrive without consistent and intentional communication.

Honesty. People in poly communities often emphasize nonviolent communication (using "I statements" and listening compassionately) and radical honesty (telling the truth even if it is not comfortable or convenient) as ways to create intimacy and work through conflict. Key to both of those practices is honesty, with self and others. Telling lies means negotiating in bad faith, a breach of poly community norms, which prize honesty above all else. Most importantly, without honesty, it is very difficult to feel safe and trust that partners will live up to safer-sex and other agreements.

Growth. Communication, honesty, and working through conflict often lead to personal growth. Having to face their insecurities, question their motives, and consider their own boundaries almost forces poly people to either get to know themselves, or leave the relationship style. Poly people who don't come to grips with their issues tend to go from one dramatic relationship explosion to the next.

Enough love to go around. When discussing their relationship style, poly people often point to an abundance of love. They sometimes compare loving multiple partners to loving multiple children. They point out that parents do not stop loving the children they have simply because they have another child. Rather, their love grows to include that new child, and still includes previous children. In that same way, poly people can still love their current partners even when they fall in love with someone else. Because poly people are able to love more than one person, sexual variety in poly relationships does not have to come at the expense of emotional intimacy. As poly lore has it, some poly people really can "have their Jake and Edith" too!

Do polyamorous relationships work?

Just like all relationships, the health of a poly relationship depends on the people involved and how they handle themselves. It's also important to think about how we decide a relationship is "successful."

If we use a traditional definition, a relationship that "works" is one where a couple gets legally married, has kids, and remains together in an emotionally intimate and sexually exclusive relationship until one of them dies. By this definition, polyamory does not work. Unfortunately, the high rates of divorce and infidelity in the United States show that most monogamous relationships do not work this way, either. When they don't work, they are called "failed" relationships or "broken" families.

If we define a successful relationship as one that meets the needs of the people involved and can be flexible as needs change, then polyamory works well for some people. These people tend to work through conflict by accepting life transitions as key elements that help their families work. If their relationships change form over time, it does not mean they have failed or are somehow broken, only that their needs and personalities have evolved. Even if two people no longer have sex, they can still co-parent effectively, rely on each other for help, and remain emotionally supportive. The flexibility inherent in polyamory provides some relationships with a unique resilience that allows them to serve the needs of adults and kids over time.

When it is good, it is very good indeed. When people have long-term poly relationships that work well for them, their lives tend to run fairly smoothly, without a lot of drama. By setting boundaries that meet everyone's needs, communicating effectively, and practicing relationship skills and techniques, these poly folks can have lasting, loving, and satisfying relationships. Many poly families live caring and happy lives in which their multiple partners multiply their happiness.

When it is bad, it is horrid. When polyamorous relationships melt down, they can do so spectacularly. If things go wrong, the consequences are not limited to the people directly involved. Mistakes and bad choices have the potential to echo through others' relationships, which is why trust is so important in polyamorous relationships.

Advantages of polyamorous relationships

The advantages people get in polyamorous relationships are similar to the motivations they list for trying polyamory.

While they like the sexual variety, most adults say that the additional emotional, financial, and practical support that comes with polyamory far outweighs any sexual advantages. For parents in poly families, sharing parenting among more than two people means more sleep and personal time for everyone.

Another advantage of poly is the freedom to be, think, and act genuinely. Poly people think deeply about what they want and purposefully create relationships outside of social norms. So for some, polyamory can be a crash course in self-knowledge and personal growth. Linking freedom with honesty allows poly people to develop deep emotional intimacy with each other. Parents who are polyamorous tend to be very honest when communicating with their children. They feel this honesty creates greater intimacy and trust among all family members.

Polyamory-specific challenges

Not every poly relationship hovers in blissful defiance of reality. Though love may be infinite, free time is often in short supply, and when time spent with one partner comes at the expense of time with another, it can lead to jealousy and hurt feelings. Some poly people deal with this by spending time together in groups so no one is excluded. Other challenges are not as easy to solve.

Jealousy

Mainstream culture in the United States is saturated with jealousy. Popular images of romance cast jealousy as an emblem of true love—because someone must really care if they are jealous, right? The other side of jealousy is so little-known that polyamorists had to make up a word for it: *compersion,* or the warm glow of happiness that comes when one's lover is happy with one of their other lovers.

Just like monogamists, most polyamorists experience jealousy at some point in their relationships. Poly people have four primary responses to jealousy, frequently moving between them (and sometimes going through all four in one evening).

Freaking out and wanting control. Often, especially when first exploring polyamory, people who experience jealousy get extremely upset and feel threatened. This feeling of threat can make the jealous person want to control others, so they create rules that limit how their partners can interact with their other partners. Rules rarely work, however, and a more effective strategy is to talk about feelings of jealousy.

Discussion and communication. Speaking openly of jealousy can help defuse the feelings. Partners can respond to the person who's feeling jealous by telling and showing them that they are loved. Experienced poly people try to focus on the emotions beneath the jealousy: often insecurity or fear of loss. By facing those fears directly, poly people are able to deal with the issues head-on instead of letting them run the show from behind the scenes.

Anticipating and overcompensating for new relationship energy. New relationship energy, or NRE, is the bubbly feeling that comes with new love. The rush of new love makes every thing related to the new love interest seem fun and exciting. In contrast, long-standing relationships can seem boring, or simply get overshadowed by the brilliance of the NRE. Practiced poly people take several steps to overcompensate for NRE, to help keep their other partners from feeling jealous. They might make sure to spend extra time and attention on longer-term relationships and to acknowledge the effects of NRE.

Compersion. Compersion is the glee of seeing one's lover falling in love with someone else. Poly people who experience compersion says it's like being happy that their partner got a part in a local theater production or was chosen employee of the month. It does not affect them directly, but they are still happy to see their partner happy and having good things happen. Practiced poly people show compersion by doing things like vacating the large bedroom for their partner to host a visiting lover, taking care of kids so their partners can go on dates, and treating their metamours kindly.

Mono/poly relationships

Poly people have to make careful agreements about what kind of relationships they want. This is especially true if one person wants a poly relationship but another person is unsure, or would like a monogamous relationship. If the monogamous person is pressured into a poly relationship, it tends to lead to disaster. Such pressure can take a range of forms: financial, emotional, physical, explicit, implied, or even unconscious. Agreements made under pressure are not truly consensual, because they come with some kind of threat. If "no" is not an acceptable answer, then "yes" is not a real choice.

A common scenario goes something like this: Chris prefers monogamy, but Kacey wants sex outside the relationship. Kacey threatens to leave if Chris demands monogamy, so Chris agrees to a poly relationship. Eventually, emotions and the stress of time management lead Chris to have a meltdown. Chris admits to never really wanting a poly relationship. Because this agreement was made under threat, it was fragile, likely to crack when tested. Such mono/poly relationships are generally not successful or happy.

Not all mono/poly relationships follow this model, though. If everyone is honest and truly open to the relationship, then these relationships can be very happy. For example, when a monogamous person with a low sex drive has been with a person who has a higher sex drive, it can create friction in the relationship, as well as guilt for the person with the lower sex drive, who sometimes comes to feel that they are depriving their beloved of a rich and satisfying sex life. Allowing the person with the higher sex drive to have other partners can be a tremendous relief, allowing the other partner some breathing room. Some even report that they actually enjoy sex a lot more once they are doing it because they really want to, and not because they feel guilty for not doing it. The people who get to keep their loving relationship with their long-term partner and explore sexual variety with others often report a feeling of freedom, excitement, and fulfillment that increases their satisfaction in their long-term relationship.

In addition to a mismatch of sexual appetites, other configurations that lend themselves to a happy poly/mono relationship are when one person is disabled and unable or too sick to have sex while the other person remains well, or when one person has a job that takes them away from home for long periods of time. In these and other cases, mono/poly relationships can be very fulfilling for those involved.

Legal problems

People who are not in traditional monogamous, heterosexual relationships are sometimes at risk of losing custody of their children. Family members (often ex-spouses, parents, or grandparents) or government child welfare services can challenge custody of children. In many jurisdictions, courts view lesbians and gay men as legitimate parents worthy of legal rights similar to those conferred on heterosexual parents. In most places, polyamorous families do not have the same rights.

When polys have to go to family court, it can matter a lot which judge gets the case and in which court, and how the judge feels about the lawyers. Family court judges have a lot of freedom, and they are driven by what they decide is in the best interest of the child. If the judge feels that polyamory is harmful to a child's health and safety, then no amount of discussion will sway that opinion.

Other legal issues poly people can face include:

- Housing laws, such as those that prohibit more than two unrelated people from living together.
- Morality clauses in employment contracts, which allow employers to fire employees for "immorality."
- Selective enforcement of adultery laws.

Because polyamory is not as well-known as other diverse relationship forms like those of gays and lesbians, poly families can often pass unnoticed, and so avoid prosecution for their relationships.

Children and polyamory

Polyamorous families can be just as healthy as other families. My and others' research shows that there is nothing inherently dysfunctional about polyamorous families, and they are not destined to damage the children who grow up in them. The effects on children of having poly parents depend in large part on how the adults act in their relationships.

I should note that the people in my study were optimistic about polyamory, and so their kids were fairly optimistic, as well. The mainstream polyamorous communities in the United States, Australia, and Western Europe are composed primarily of white, middle-class, highly educated people. Like other middle-class white people, poly parents pass their race and class privilege on to their children. For example, kids whose parents have multiple graduate degrees (about two-thirds of the adults in my study had at least a masters degree, and almost half had a PhD) are already starting off with many advantages compared with children whose parents have less education. However, I feel that what I learned from these kids provides an accurate description of what kids experience in many poly families.

Advantages for children in poly families

Poly families are not perfect, and family life for all the kids in my study was a mix of ups and downs of the same kind you'll find in any family. But for those poly folks who can find the right balance in their relationships, multiple-adult families can offer children many benefits.

The children in my study are generally in great shape: They are articulate and intelligent, outgoing and thoughtful, poised and self-confident. Several of them mentioned how the freedom to think and ask questions, and to expect a truthful and thoughtful answer, had allowed them to explore their own ideas. They expected their parents to support their questioning, and this led them to have a strong self-image.

It really does take a village. Multiple adults provide more attention, life experience, support, and role models for children. Pooling their resources also allows adults to have more personal time, work more flexible hours, and get more sleep, because there are multiple people around to take care of the children. Poly parents said that they felt more patient and had more energy for their children when they were well-rested and had enough income—which in turn benefitted their children.

Children in poly families also said they liked the extra resources in the family. Kids in my study told me they liked having more people to ask for advice, money, help with homework, and rides. Several children said their parents' partners provided different role models. They also felt that these adults helped family life go more smoothly, because their parents got to see alternative methods of discipline and communication.

The biggest complaint kids in my study had was that they couldn't get away with anything, because there were too many adults paying attention. Even "worse" (in the kids' view), the adults all communicated with each other, so any lie that the kids told to one adult had to remain consistent over multiple tellings to different adults.

Talking about polyamory

How parents talk to their kids about polyamory makes a big difference to how the kids will feel about their parents' relationships. For kids of all ages, the best strategy seems to be an age-appropriate and honest response to kids' questions. How old the children are also makes a big difference in what they think of the adults in their families.

I did not interview kids under five years old, but I did observe them, and they seemed very much like other middle-class white children I had observed in other family settings. Little kids take their family form for granted, because it is all they know. Until they learn that other peoples' families are different, they will not think that their family is unusual. These very young kids might not need an explanation about poly at all.

In my study, kids between five and eight years old often did not think their families were much different from their friends' families. They also did not think their parents' partners were unusual. Rather, parents' partners blended in with the other adults who cared for them, including grandparents, aunts, uncles, friends, and babysitters. Children under 10 years old usually have early bedtimes, so kids miss the adult-only interaction that happens later. Because the adults don't usually make a big deal out of their partners, these younger kids don't think much about these "extra" adults.

Children between nine and twelve years old from poly families start noticing that their families are different. While they may have noticed differences before and not thought much about them, tweens have a much better understanding of their social surroundings. They might notice looks or touches between adults in ways their younger siblings do not. At this stage, many kids from poly families will ask questions, and parents will then answer them with age-appropriate truth.

Kids might be concerned that their parents are cheating, and so might think they know a terrible secret that will hurt the other parent. In those cases, it is important for parents to let kids know that the parents are being honest with each other, there is no secret from the other parent, and the kids can ask whatever questions they have. Kids in these settings often do not want detailed explanations of the romantic side of things. Phrases like "hanging out" or "spending special time together" can be honest answers appropriate for younger tweens.

Teens between 13 and 17 years old have to do the most work to manage the information about their polyamorous families with friends, teachers, friends' parents, and other adults. Their peers are more sophisticated and more observant of adult relationships, and they sometimes even figure out on their own that some adults are non-monogamous.

All teens are busy figuring out their individual identities, and puberty often brings feelings of attraction for others. Teens from poly families have the added complication of trying to figure out their own sexualities when coming from a family with some sexual non-conformists. One teen in my sample was sure that he would be polyamorous, and another was sure that she would not be. The rest did not know, and said that they were just figuring things out and had not thought that far ahead yet. One thing is clear: kids from poly families do not assume that they will be poly when they grow up. They know that they can make a choice (or many different choices) when they are older.

Protecting the kids

You might be worried that your loved one's children will be hurt by their parents' polyamory. They may be discriminated against or hurt when one of their parents' relationships ends. In most cases, loving poly parents work hard to make sure their kids are safe from judgment, discrimination, and emotional pain.

Most people have either never heard of polyamory or don't know much about it, so they probably don't even think about the possibility that they know a poly family. If you see a woman and two men sitting at a table in a restaurant, you might think they are a couple with their friend before it occurs to you that they might be a polyamorous triad. Polyamory is not on most people's minds, so kids and other family members rarely have to explain their families at all.

Divorce is so common in modern American society that multiple parents—for example, mom and her second (or third) husband, plus dad and his new boyfriend—are common. Kids in poly families say that friends, teachers, and other adults usually assume that the kids are from divorced families that get along well. Most of the time, the kids just let people believe whatever story they make up for themselves. Sometimes the kids will tell friends whom they trust. In short, if they want to, kids from poly families can almost always hide the fact that their families are polyamorous.

When poly relationships grow, it's likely that people will come and go. It makes sense: the bigger the group, the more likely it is that someone will leave or others will join. What happens when the group includes children who become attached to adults, and those beloved adults are the ones who leave? When I asked kids about the disadvantages of living in a poly family, I thought they would talk about the pain they felt when parents' partners left. Instead, I was surprised to find that missing parents' partners was far down the disadvantage list, well behind crowded houses and younger siblings taking or going through older siblings' private stuff.

However, some kids in my study said they felt quite upset when their parents broke up with partners whom the children had come to love. The kids missed their former adult companions, and they sometimes compared parents' new partners with others they had known and loved before. Some even refused to get close to new partners because of the old hurt from having earlier bonded with an adult who then left.

Forming family ties

Like divorced parents and others who form blended families, poly parents use a number of strategies to lessen the impact of their dating on their children. Parents in poly relationships use extreme caution when introducing new partners, and do so only quite slowly. They use strategies like meeting partners outside of the home, dating for a long period of time before having sex, asking around poly communities about their prospective partners' previous relationships, and in some cases even doing background checks. As a result, many children are not even aware when some partners leave, because they never met those people in the first place.

Because poly people are often quite social, they tend to interact with lots of friends and community members. With all of these people around, parents' partners can blend in to the social background, and so often don't stand out in children's lives. Parental sexuality is often irrelevant to (especially younger) children, because it happens behind closed doors. As relationships deepen, people spend more time together, and eventually it becomes clear to the children when a partner is particularly significant. Parents generally wait until their relationships have lasted long enough that people are emotionally committed to each other before allowing partners to stand out to their children as family members.

In many poly communities, the ideal is for adults to bond with children and continue that link even if the various adults no longer have a relationship. In this idyllic vision, adults and children form lasting emotional connections that are independent of any other relationships. When breakups are especially hurtful, it can become difficult for adults to live up to this ideal, and in those cases, kids and former partners often lose touch with each other. In other cases, poly adults can transition from romantic relationships to friendships or polyaffective (emotionally intimate and platonic) relationships and mutually help the children spend time with valued adults.

Children in poly families often observe their parents cherishing emotional connections that are outside of conventional relationship forms, where people rely on biological or legal links to determine who is a "real" family member. Following suit, such children often build their own connections with people, completely independent of their parents' social lives. By forging emotionally intimate relationships based on mutual reliance and support, kids and parents in poly families expand beyond biological or legal kinship into what scholars call *chosen kinship* (something common among many gender and sexual minorities). In this way, children in poly families can take charge of constructing their own chosen families and social circles.

Polyamory and sexual health

Having multiple partners increases the risk of sexually transmitted infections (STIs), and one person's exposure can mean exposure of others down the line. How do people in polyamorous relationships deal with this magnified risk of STIs? Very carefully.

True to polyamorous form, which emphasizes communication as a key relationship tool, poly folks talk with each other, and often with their partners' partners, about STIs. Most often, people get tested (often with six-month follow ups) and come together for a conversation about their results. This is often a "show and tell," where everyone sits in a circle, handing printed results around. It makes a difference to see the people who will be affected by your sexual choices and to speak to them directly about how everyone is going to protect each other's health.

Condoms and dental dams can go a long way toward cutting the transmission of STIs by containing fluids and preventing (or at least inhibiting) skin-to-skin contact. There are also many ways to have sex or sexual interactions that do not involve fluid exchange, and poly people can be creative about what kinds of sex they have and how they do it.

Because STIs can spread through a social group, most mainstream poly networks have strict agreements concerning *fluid bonding*, or the exchange of bodily fluids other than saliva. These agreements often don't allow fluid bonding until all partners have had a chance to discuss it and get tested for STIs. This can be such an extensive process that actually deciding to have unprotected sex is a sign of serious commitment, sometimes even associated with commitment ceremonies.

How does all of this careful talking, testing, and negotiating work for poly folks? Pretty darn well, it turns out. A recent study showed that people participating in negotiated non-monogamy have fewer STIs and infect fewer partners than do people who are cheating and have not negotiated multiple-partner sexuality. In the study, openly non-monogamous folks were more likely to get tested for STIs often, discuss their sexual health status with partners, and use condoms and other barriers than were people who had not negotiated an open relationship. Cheaters were less likely to use condoms, get tested for STIs, or discuss safer-sex concerns with new partners.

Living polyamorously in a monogamous world

Some people in easily recognized forms of relationships might find it hard to understand why polyamorists or other sexual minorities feel the need to come out. "Why can't they leave it in the bedroom, like everyone else does?" But most monogamous people don't just leave their relationships "in the bedroom." People talk about their family members or significant others when discussing what they did over the weekend, their vacation plans, or who is coming for dinner. For poly people (or any sexual minority), it can be painful, humiliating, and exhausting to leave out relationship information that others share freely in the course of social conversation. Hiding relationships from close friends or families of origin also implies that polyamorous relationships are bad or shameful, a message many poly parents do not want to give children.

In other cases, poly people prefer to keep their romantic or intimate lives private, and that is acceptable as well. If your loved one is disclosing this information to you, then clearly they wish for you to have it. That might not mean that they wish for everyone, in every circumstance, to have that same information. Sometimes it is just not relevant. It is best to discuss this idea with your loved ones to see how they wish to handle it.

When poly people come out, that does not mean that they want to date every other person they meet. Most poly people want to date only other poly people, and are not interested in "recruiting" monogamous people to date polyamorously, because that is often a recipe for disaster. People who are truly monogamous tend to be unhappy in polyamorous arrangements, so people looking for poly relationships tend to look elsewhere.

Supporting polyamorous loved ones

There are a few ways to support loved ones who have come out as polyamorous.

Communicating honestly will help all of you to express your feelings and ideas. Your poly loved one will be knee-deep in developing additional communication skills as they navigate multiple-partner relationships, and those skills can (ideally) help them communicate with non-poly loved ones as well.

Honesty does not have to be brutal, though, and all people involved should treat each other with compassion and communicate with each other's best interests at heart. Being kind in the face of fear and discomfort can be difficult, but when everyone involved strives for kindness, it is easier for everyone to attain it.

Don't blame all their problems on polyamory. Poly people report that their non-polyamorous friends, family, and counselors often do this. This can be true of problems that have nothing to do with polyamory at all. Since it is unusual, polyamory becomes the universal scapegoat for all relationship issues, and non-poly people can have a hard time recognizing other issues. Consider that you wouldn't blame a monogamous person's troubles on monogamy—it's no different with polyamory.

Blended families of all sorts deal with a wide range of issues, most of which have nothing to do with parental sexuality or relationship status. Far more family challenges are related to family dynamics, money, housework, discipline, and so on. These mundane family issues *are* sometimes made more complex by polyamorous relationships, simply because there are more people involved, expressing more opinions. In other cases, the extra support actually simplifies family life by helping financially, practically, or personally.

Finally, include everyone in events and holidays. When you see poly family members at holidays and events, use the same courtesy and discretion you would use with other family members. If something specific comes up—seating arrangements at a wedding, for instance—discuss with your poly loved ones how they would like to handle it. Include poly partners as you would other members of the family in gift-giving and invitations to events.

Talking to other people about your loved one's poly relationships

Research shows that when gay or lesbian people come out to their families of origin, sometimes those family members feel like they are the ones who end up "in the closet" and have difficulty explaining their gay or lesbian relative to friends and family. While your poly loved one may feel a tremendous sense of relief after being open with you, you might feel uncomfortable when you consider how to explain it to other relatives.

There are a few ways you can handle it. First, discuss it with your poly loved one. What does your loved one want, or think of the situation? Some people don't mind if Mom or Dad tells the family about their polyamorous kids, but others want to be able to tell the news themselves. Before speaking with anyone about your poly loved one's romantic life, find out what level of privacy that loved one wants.

Chat with your poly loved ones about what to say if people ask directly about their partners: Is it okay to say that person is a friend? Should you direct the questioner to speak directly with the poly person? Or would they prefer you speak openly about it? Some poly people prefer this, as an indication that you support their choices and are not ashamed of them.

As I already mentioned, many people do not recognize polyamorous relationships. Telling these people about your poly loved one might add a lot of stress and tension to your family, so sometimes it might be best to adopt a "don't ask, don't tell" policy, and not discuss it with them unless it becomes necessary. This might be the case if the person is a distant relative, or someone you or the poly person do not often see. In some cases, your poly loved one might have specific family members they don't want to share their relationships with.

If you and your poly loved one have decided that it is appropriate or important to explain polyamory to friends or family members, consider using this pamphlet to help start the discussion.

Polyamory and religion

Among organized religions, attitudes towards polyamory vary from extreme discomfort and distaste to complete acceptance. At one end of that spectrum, conservative or fundamentalist sects of Christianity, Islam, and Judaism forbid sex outside marriage and base family on a strict sexual exclusivity. At the other end of the spectrum, the Unitarian Universalists, pagans, various New Age religions, and people who practice sacred sexuality of several varieties celebrate a multiplicity of gods and lovers. In between lies a wide range of beliefs advocating greater or lesser amounts of tolerance or acceptance. The more liberal and sex-positive a religion is, the more likely it will accept polyamorous people.

The "Big Three" in the United States—Christianity, Islam, and Judaism—share the same beliefs that require heterosexuality and marriage to create children. All three accept sexuality within religiously recognized unions and discourage sex outside of marriage. Christianity tends to have stricter teachings about sexual pleasure than either Judaism or Islam. None of the conservative sects of the Big Three encourage their followers to practice polyamory. However, some liberal wings of Judaism and Christianity are less restrictive and may allow, or at least not explicitly condemn, polyamory.

If you're concerned about how polyamory fits in with your religious beliefs, I suggest you turn to an advisor such as a priest or pastor for help.

I'm really struggling with this. What can I do?

It's okay for you to take time to process this information. Ask your poly loved one for some space if you need it. Take a look at the resources section for some more in-depth material that can help you understand polyamory. It might also be a good idea for you to speak with a therapist to help you work through your feelings. If you are upset now, don't assume you will stay upset over the long term. Research on gays and lesbians who come out to their families shows that the family members often feel a greater sense of comfort and relaxation over issues of sexual orientation over time, because the shock of the information fades, and mundane interactions with family members help things return to something like they were before disclosure.

It's important to remember that people can have happy, loving, and fulfilling polyamorous relationships—sometimes far happier than their monogamous relationships were. The relationship style might not work for you, but that doesn't mean it's exploitative or hurtful to your polyamorous loved one, or the people they love. Polyamory can provide people with more love, affection, attention, and expanded personal horizons that contribute to self-growth and personal contentment. I hope that with time and understanding, you will come to accept and embrace this newly discovered facet of your loved one.

Glossary and resources

chosen kinship: family that you choose, rather than the family you were born into (biological) or a family you married into (legal)

compersion: the fuzzy feeling a poly person gets when they see one of their partners being happy with another partner

dyad: a two-person relationship

fluid bonding: sharing bodily fluids other than saliva during sex; if two people are fluid bonded, it usually means they have sex without barriers like condoms

metamour: a partner's partner

monogamy: a relationship style where two people have no other sexual or romantic partners

new relationship energy (NRE): the emotional high you feel at the beginning of a relationship

non-monogamy: any type of relationship style that is not based on two people being romantically and/or sexually exclusive

polyaffective relationships: non-sexual, emotionally intimate relationships between people who share a polyamorous partner but are not lovers themselves

polyamory: a relationship style where people have more than one partner with the full knowledge and consent of all their partners

polyfidelitous relationships: polyamorous relationships where two or more people are sexually exclusive

polygamy: a relationship style where someone is married to more than one person

quad: four people who are connected through romantic ties to one another, who may all be involved with each other, or may only be involved with one or two others in the group

triad: three people who are all romantically involved with one another (distinct from a "vee," below)

vee: a three-person arrangement where two people are involved with a third person, known as the "pivot," but not with each other

Books

More Than Two: A Practical Guide to Ethical Polyamory, by Franklin Veaux and Eve Rickert. Thorntree Press, 2014.

The Polyamorists Next Door: Inside Multiple-Partner Relationships and Families, by Elisabeth Sheff. Rowman & Littlefield, 2013.

Ask Me About Polyamory! The Best of Kimchi Cuddles, by Tikva Wolf. Thorntree Press, 2016.

Stories from the Polycule: Real Life in Polyamorous Families, an anthology edited by Elisabeth Sheff. Thorntree Press, 2015.

The Ethical Slut: A Practical Guide to Polyamory, Open Relationships & Other Adventures, second edition, by Dossie Easton and Janet Hardy. Celestial Arts, 2009.

The Jealousy Workbook: Exercises and Insights for Managing Open Relationships, by Kathy Labriola. Greenery Press, 2013.

Groups and organizations
Loving More, lovemore.com
The Polyamory Society, polyamorysociety.org
Alt.Polyamory, polyamory.org/SF/groups.html
Unitarian Universalists for Polyamory Awareness,
www.uupa.org
Polyfamilies,
groups.yahoo.com/neo/groups/polyfamilies/info

Blogs
Poly in the News, polyinthemedia.blogspot.com
Elisabeth Sheff's personal blog, elisabethsheff.com
Elisabeth Sheff's blog on Psychology Today,
psychologytoday.com/blog/the-polyamorists-next-door
More Than Two website and blog, morethantwo.com
Polyamory Paradigm, polyamoryparadigm.blogspot.com
Reverend Beverly Dale,
www.beverlydale.org/hot_topics/polyamory